SPECTRUM®

Telling Time

Grade 1

Published by Spectrum®
an imprint of Carson-Dellosa Publishing
Greensboro, NC

Spectrum®
An imprint of Carson-Dellosa Publishing LLC
P.O. Box 35665
Greensboro, NC 27425 USA

Printed in the USA • All rights reserved.   ISBN 978-1-4838-3109-1
01-053167784

Table of Contents Telling Time

NAME _____

Check What You Know

Calendar Skills

These are the days of the week. They are in the wrong order.
Write 2–7 to put the days of the week in the right order.

Sunday	Friday	Thursday	Tuesday	Wednesday	Saturday	Monday

___1___   _____   _____   _____   _____   _____   _____

Write the month that comes before or after.

February   _____   April

June   July   _____

October   November   _____

Look at the calendar for this week.

Sunday	Monday	Tuesday	Wednesday	Thursday	Friday	Saturday
1	2 baseball game	3 Miguel's birthday	4	5 piano practice	6	7

Circle the day of the week that
Brent has a baseball game.   Monday   Thursday

Circle the day of the week that
Miguel's birthday is on.   Sunday   Tuesday

NAME _____

Check What You Know

Calendar Skills

Look at the calendar for September.

SEPTEMBER

Sunday	Monday	Tuesday	Wednesday	Thursday	Friday	Saturday
				1 school	2	3 swim lessons
4	5	6	7	8	9	10 swim lessons
11	12	13	14	15	16	17 swim lessons
18	19 painting	20	21	22	23	24 swim lessons
25	26	27	28	29	30	

Circle the day of the week for swim lessons.   Sunday   Saturday

Circle the date that school starts.   September 1   September 12

Circle the date the family will paint.   September 23   September 19

Lesson 1.1 Identifying Days of the Week

There are seven days in a week.

The days of the week are always in this order:

Sunday Monday Tuesday Wednesday Thursday Friday Saturday

Put the train cars in the order of the days of the week.
Trace and write 1–7.

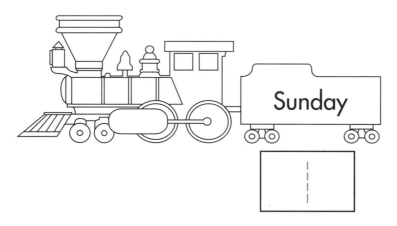

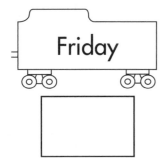

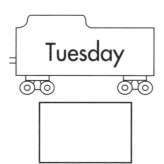

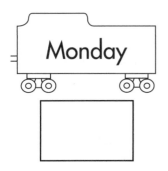

Lesson 1.1 Identifying Days of the Week

The days of the week are shown on a calendar.
Say the days of the week.

Sunday	Monday	Tuesday	Wednesday	Thursday	Friday	Saturday

The days repeat each week. Sundays are colored red. Color Mondays blue. Color Tuesdays yellow. Color Wednesdays green. Color Thursdays purple. Color Fridays pink. Color Saturdays orange.

Lesson 1.2 Identifying Months of the Year

There are 12 months in the year.

The months of the year are always in this order:

January	February	March
April	May	June
July	August	September
October	November	December

Put the months in the correct order. Trace and write 1–12.

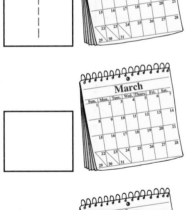

Lesson 1.2 Identifying Months of the Year

Say the months of the year:

January   February   March   April   May   June

July   August   September   October   November   December

Write the month that comes before or after.

_____   October   November

May   _____   July

February   March   _____

August   September   _____

July   _____   September

_____   June   July

Lesson 1.3 Reading a Calendar

Look at Sam's calendar. Tell what is happening this week.

Sunday	Monday	Tuesday	Wednesday	Thursday	Friday	Saturday
1 library	2 softball practice	3 Miguel's birthday	4	5	6 doctor appointment	7

On what day does Sam play softball?

_____

On what day does Sam celebrate his friend's birthday?

_____

On what day does Sam go to the library?

_____

On what day does Sam play the piano?

_____

On what day does Sam go to the doctor?

doctor

_____

On what days does Sam have nothing to do?

_____ and _____

NAME _____

Lesson 1.3 Reading a Calendar

Look at Bella's calendars. Tell what is happening each month.

APRIL

Sunday	Monday	Tuesday	Wednesday	Thursday	Friday	Saturday
1	2	3	4	5	6	7
8	9	10	11	12	13	14
15	16	17	18	19	20	21
22 29	23 30	24	25	22	27	28

JULY

Sunday	Monday	Tuesday	Wednesday	Thursday	Friday	Saturday
1	2	3	4	5	6	7
8	9	10	11	12	13	14
15	16	17	18	19	20	21
22 29	23 30	24 31	25	22	27	28

SEPTEMBER

Sunday	Monday	Tuesday	Wednesday	Thursday	Friday	Saturday
1	2	3	4	5	6	7
8	9	10	11	12	13	14
15	16	17	18	19	20	21
22 29	23 30	24	25	22	27	28

In what month does Bella celebrate her birthday?

_____

In what month does Bella start school?

_____

In what month does Bella go to the beach?

_____

Lesson 1.3 Reading a Calendar

Mom plans family activities for July. Answer the questions.

JULY

Sunday	Monday	Tuesday	Wednesday	Thursday	Friday	Saturday
				1	2	3 camp
4	5	6	7 game night	8	9	10
11	12 zoo	13	14 game night	15	16	17
18	19	20	21 game night	22 karate	23	24
25	26	27	28 game night	29	30	31

When is game night?	Friday	Wednesday
When is karate?	Tuesday	Thursday
When is camping?	July 13	July 3
When is the trip to the zoo?	July 12	July 20

Lesson 1.4 Using a Calendar

Josie has swimming lessons on Monday. She has singing lessons on Friday. Help Josie plan the rest of her week by following the directions below.

Sunday	Monday	Tuesday	Wednesday	Thursday	Friday	Saturday
	swim lessons				singing lessons	

Josie wants to play kickball with her friends.

On the calendar, draw a ball on the day Josie will play kickball.

Write the day Josie will play kickball. _____

Josie wants to practice her dance moves with Dan.

On the calendar, write the word **dance** on the day

Josie will practice dancing.

Write the day Josie will practice dancing. _____

Josie wants to write a story.

On the calendar, draw a pencil on the day Josie will write a story.

Write the day Josie will write a story. _____

Check What You Learned

Calendar Skills

Write the missing days of the week.

_____, Monday, _____,

_____, _____, Friday,

_____

Write the month that comes before or after.

_____ November December

January February _____

Look at Tom's calendar.

FEBRUARY

Sunday	Monday	Tuesday	Wednesday	Thursday	Friday	Saturday
1	2	3	4	5	6	7
8	9	10	11	12	13	14
15	16	17	18	19	20	21
22	23	24	25	22	27	28

When will Tom leave on a trip?

Saturday   Sunday

When will Tom go to a party?

February 9   February 19

CHAPTER 1 POSTTEST

NAME _____

 # Check What You Know

Time of Day

Label each event with the time of day it is most likely to happen. Use **M** for morning, **A** for afternoon, **E** for evening, and **N** for night.

_____ Everyone sleeps.

_____ Families eat breakfast.

_____ Stars come out in the sky.

_____ School buses take children to school.

_____ The sun goes down.

_____ Children come home from school.

Circle the time that best completes each sentence.

I had a doctor's appointment at _____ in the morning. The sun was just rising.   one o'clock   ten o'clock

The first graders ate lunch at _____ in the afternoon.   twelve thirty   five o'clock

The play started at _____ in the evening.   two thirty   seven thirty

Clara went to bed at _____ at night.   five o'clock   nine o'clock

Lesson 2.1 Understanding Time of Day: Morning

Morning is the beginning of the day.

The sun comes up in the morning.

People wake up in the morning.

Circle the events that often happen in the morning.

Children come home from school.   Alarm clocks ring.

Everyone gets ready for bed.   Families eat breakfast.

School buses take children to school.   Adults leave for work.

Draw a picture of something you do in the morning.

Lesson 2.2 Understanding Time of Day: Afternoon

Afternoon is the part of the day between morning and when the sun sets.

The sun is still in the sky in the afternoon.

People eat lunch in the afternoon.

Circle the events that often happen in the afternoon.

Students go out for recess.

Children come home from school.

People wake up.

Teachers teach lessons.

Children have play dates.

Adults leave for work.

Draw a picture of something you do in the afternoon.

Lesson 2.3 Understanding Time of Day: Evening

Evening is near the end of the day.

The sun goes down in the evening.

Families often spend time indoors in the evening.

Circle the events that often happen in the evening.

People eat dinner.   People eat breakfast.

Families play board games.   Children do homework.

Children play tag.   Alarm clocks ring.

Draw a picture of something you do in the evening.

Lesson 2.4 Understanding Time of Day: Night

Night is at the very end of the day.

The sky is dark at night.

People sleep at night.

Circle the events that often happen at night.

Parents read to children.   Adults make breakfast.

Stores close for the day.   Stars come out in the sky.

Children play sports.   Teachers teach lessons.

Draw a picture of something you do in the evening.

Lesson 2.5 Understanding Clock Time With Time of Day

When telling time, it is important to know what part of the day it is, too. That's because we use each time twice a day. For example, we have 4:00 in the morning and 4:00 in the afternoon. Very different things are likely to happen at those two times of day.

four o'clock in the morning

four o'clock in the afternoon

What do you do at each time? Write your answer on the line.

At twelve thirty in the afternoon, I _____.

At twelve thirty at night, I _____.

At seven o'clock in the morning, I _____.

At seven o'clock in the evening, I _____.

Lesson 2.6 Combining Clock Time With Time of Day

Circle the time of day that fits best with the event described.

Breakfast is served at six thirty _____.

in the morning   in the evening

The sun goes down at five thirty _____.

in the morning   in the evening

My family goes to the beach at
two o'clock _____.

in the afternoon   at night

Eli gets ready for bed at eight o'clock
_____.

in the morning   at night

Our class has spelling lessons at
one thirty _____.

in the afternoon   at night

Lesson 2.6 Combining Clock Time With Time of Day

Finish each sentence. Then, draw a picture
of something you do at that time.

At _seven o'clock_
in the morning, I

_____.

At _____
in the afternoon, I

_____.

At _____
in the evening, I

_____.

At _____
at night, I

_____.

Check What You Learned

Time of Day

Label each event with the time of day it is most likely to happen.
Use **M** for morning, **A** for afternoon, **E** for evening, and **N** for night.

_____ Families eat dinner.   _____ Alarm clocks ring.

_____ The moon shines brightly.   _____ Students eat lunch.

_____ Adults leave for work.   _____ Children come home
                                          from school.

Circle the time that best completes each sentence.

Grandma got up at _____ in the morning.
The sun was just rising.

six thirty   nine thirty   twelve thirty

Jerome had soccer practice at _____ in the afternoon.

three o'clock   six o'clock   eleven o'clock

Uncle Peter played tennis until _____ in the evening.

three thirty   seven thirty   ten thirty

Sasha woke up in the middle of the night. It was _____.

six o'clock   eight o'clock   twelve o'clock

NAME _____

Check What You Know

Reading Clocks

Circle the time for each clock.

nine o'clock   eleven o'clock

ten o'clock   two o'clock

three o'clock   four o'clock

eight o'clock   seven o'clock

six thirty   seven thirty

twelve thirty   one thirty

five thirty   six thirty

ten thirty   nine thirty

NAME _____

 Check What You Know

Reading Clocks

Read the clocks. Write the times in two ways.

The time is _____ o'clock.

_____:00

_____ thirty

_____:30

The time is _____ o'clock.

_____:00

nine _____

9:_____

Read the clock. Circle the clock that tells the same time.

Read the clock. Circle the clock that tells the same time.

Lesson 3.1 Reading Digital Clocks to the Hour

This clock tells the time. The time is eleven o'clock.

Circle the time for each clock.

   nine o'clock
four o'clock

   nine o'clock
two o'clock

   twelve o'clock
two o'clock

   one o'clock
twelve o'clock

Read the clock. Write the time.

_____ o'clock

_____ o'clock

_____ o'clock

_____ o'clock

Lesson 3.2 Reading Analog Clocks to the Hour

This clock tells the time. The time is three o'clock.

Circle the time for each clock.

   eleven o'clock

four o'clock

   five o'clock

seven o'clock

   one o'clock

twelve o'clock

   eleven o'clock

six o'clock

Read the clock. Write the time.

The time is

_____ o'clock.

The time is

_____ o'clock.

The time is

_____ o'clock.

The time is

_____ o'clock.

Lesson 3.3 Reading Digital Clocks to the Half Hour

This clock tells the time. The time is three thirty.

Circle the time for each clock.

   seven thirty

                one thirty

   three thirty

                ten thirty

   four thirty

                six thirty

   nine thirty

                eight thirty

Read the clock. Write the time.

_____ thirty

seven _____

two _____

_____ thirty

Lesson 3.4 Reading Analog Clocks to the Half Hour

This clock tells the time. The time is one thirty.

Circle the time for each clock.

   two thirty

three thirty

   five thirty

six thirty

   ten thirty

twelve thirty

   twelve thirty

two thirty

Read the clock. Write the time.

The time is

_____ thirty.

The time is

eleven _____.

The time is

eight _____.

The time is

_____ thirty.

Lesson 3.5 Reading Digital Clocks

Look at the clocks.

The time is three o'clock.

The time is three thirty.

Circle the time for each clock.

one o'clock   four o'clock

one o'clock   ten o'clock

ten thirty   one thirty

six thirty   seven thirty

Read the clock. Write the time.

_____ o'clock

_____ o'clock

_____ thirty

five _____

Lesson 3.6 Reading Analog Clocks

Look at the clocks.

The time is two o'clock.

The time is two thirty.

Circle the time for each clock.

twelve o'clock   six o'clock

eight o'clock   nine o'clock

two thirty   three thirty

six thirty   five thirty

Read the clock. Write the time.

_____ o'clock

_____ o'clock

twelve _____

_____ thirty

Lesson 3.7 Reading Digital and Analog Clocks to the Hour

Read the clock. Circle the clock that tells the same time.

Read the clock. Circle the clock that tells the same time.

Read the clock. Circle the clock that tells the same time.

Lesson 3.7 Reading Digital and Analog Clocks to the Hour

Read the clock. Circle the clock that tells the same time.

Read the clock. Circle the clock that tells the same time.

Read the clock. Circle the clock that tells the same time.

Lesson 3.7 Reading Digital and Analog Clocks to the Hour

Read the time on the first clock. Draw the hands to show this time on the second clock.

Lesson 3.7 Reading Digital and Analog Clocks to the Hour

Read the time on the first clock. Write this time on the second clock.

  |

  |

  |

  |

Lesson 3.7 Reading Digital and Analog Clocks to the Hour

Read the time on the first clock. Draw the hands to show this time on the second clock.

Read the time on the first clock. Write this time on the second clock.

Lesson 3.7 Reading Digital and Analog Clocks to the Hour

Read the time on the first clock. Draw the hands to show this time on the second clock. Then, write the time in two ways.

It is _____ o'clock.   It is _____ o'clock.

_____:00   _____:00

Read the time on the first clock. Write this time on the second clock. Then, write the time in two ways.

It is _____ o'clock.   It is _____ o'clock.

_____:00   _____:00

Lesson 3.8 Reading Digital and Analog Clocks to the Half Hour

Read the clock. Circle the clock that tells the same time.

Read the clock. Circle the clock that tells the same time.

Read the clock. Circle the clock that tells the same time.

Lesson 3.8 Reading Digital and Analog Clocks to the Half Hour

Read the clock. Circle the clock that tells the same time.

Read the clock. Circle the clock that tells the same time.

Read the clock. Circle the clock that tells the same time.

Lesson 3.8 Reading Digital and Analog Clocks to the Half Hour

Read the time on the first clock. Draw the hands to show this time on the second clock.

NAME _____

Lesson 3.8 Reading Digital and Analog Clocks to the Half Hour

Read the time on the first clock. Write this time on the second clock.

Lesson 3.8 Reading Digital and Analog Clocks to the Half Hour

Read the time on the first clock. Draw the hands to show this time on the second clock.

Read the time on the first clock. Write this time on the second clock.

Lesson 3.8 Reading Digital and Analog Clocks to the Half Hour

Read the time on the first clock. Draw the hands to show this time on the second clock. Then, write the time in two ways.

It is _____ thirty.   It is six _____.

_____:30   6:_____

Read the time on the first clock. Write this time on the second clock. Then, write the time in two ways.

It is eleven _____.   It is _____ thirty.

11:_____   _____:30

Check What You Learned

Reading Clocks

Circle the time for each clock.

four o'clock   five o'clock

two o'clock   twelve o'clock

nine o'clock   eight o'clock

one o'clock   eleven o'clock

four thirty   six thirty

five thirty   six thirty

two thirty   three thirty

five thirty   three thirty

CHAPTER 3 POSTTEST

Check What You Learned

Reading Clocks

Read the clocks. Write the times in two ways.

The time is _____ o'clock.

_____:00

The time is _____ o'clock.

_____:00

_____ thirty

_____:30

ten _____

10:_____

Read the clock. Circle the clock that tells the same time.

Read the clock. Circle the clock that tells the same time.

Mid-Test Chapters 1–3

Use Lynn's calendar to answer the questions.

JULY

Sunday		Tuesday	Wednesday		Friday	Saturday
				1	2	3
4	5	6	7	8	9	10
11	12	13	14	15	16	17
18	19	20	21	22	23	24
25	26	27	28	29	30	31

1. Write **Monday** and **Thursday** on the calendar.

2. Circle the month that comes after July.   September   August

3. Circle the day of the week that Lynn goes swimming.   Sunday   Saturday

4. Circle the date that Lynn goes to the beach.   July 4   July 16

Mid-Test Chapters 1–3

Circle the time of day that fits best with the event described.

The sun comes up at six thirty _____.

in the morning   in the evening

Dinner is served at six o'clock _____.

in the morning   in the evening

The first graders eat lunch at twelve thirty
_____.

in the afternoon   at night

We roast marshmallows at nine o'clock
_____.

in the morning   at night

My family goes bowling at one o'clock
_____.

in the afternoon   at night

Mid-Test Chapters 1–3

Circle the time for each clock.

 two o'clock
three o'clock

 ten thirty
one thirty

 seven o'clock
eight o'clock

 six thirty
five thirty

Read the clock. Circle the clock that tells the same time.

Read the clock. Circle the clock that tells the same time.

Read the time on the first clock. Show this time on the second clock.

NAME _____

Check What You Know

Reading About Time

Read the sentence. Write the time.

Sam's soccer game begins at 2:30.   _____ thirty

The school bell rings at 3:00.   three _____

Mom goes to work at 6:30.   six _____

Read the sentence. Show the time on the clock.

The movie begins at 4:00.   Dad makes dinner at 5:30.

Read the story and the questions. Show the answers on the clocks.

Juan meets his friends at 1:30 at the park. They play baseball until 3:30. Then, Juan has a snack at 4:00. Dad makes dinner. The family eats at 6:30.

What time does Juan meet his friends?   What time does Juan have a snack?

Lesson 4.1 Reading Sentences About Time

Read the sentence. Write the time.

Jan goes to school at 8:00.   _____ o'clock

Dad gets home from work at 5:30.   _____ thirty

We eat lunch at 12:00.   twelve _____

Tony has a soccer game at 9:00.   _____ o'clock

We eat dinner at 6:30.   six _____

Mom has yoga at 10:30.   _____ thirty

The library closes at 8:30.   eight _____

The party is at 3:00.   three _____

Lesson 4.1 Reading Sentences About Time

Read the sentence. Show the time on the clock.

Mom goes to work at 9:00.

Felix gets on the bus at 8:30.

Tina has swim lessons at 4:30.

Gym class begins at 2:00.

Ben takes the dog for a walk at 6:00.

Hannah takes a bath at 7:30.

The baseball game begins at 1:00.

The parade ends at 11:30.

Lesson 4.2 Reading Paragraphs About Time

Read the story and the questions. Circle the answers.

Mark and Mom have a busy day. They get up at 7:00 in the morning. Mom packs their lunch to eat at the beach. Mark gets his beach toys to play with in the afternoon. Mark and Mom get into the car at 10:30. Off to the beach they go! They tell Dad they will see him for dinner at 5:00 in the evening. Mark will go to bed by 8:30.

What time do Mark and Mom get up?	5:00	8:30	7:00
What time will Mark and Mom see Dad?	5:00	10:30	6:00
During which time of day will Mark play with the beach toys?	noon	afternoon	evening
What time do Mark and Mom leave for the beach?	6:00	8:30	10:30
During which time of day will the family eat dinner?	evening	night	afternoon
What time will Mark go to bed?	10:30	8:30	6:00

Lesson 4.2 Reading Paragraphs About Time

Read the story and the questions. Show the answers on the clocks.

Jason loves going to school. His alarm rings at 6:00. By 6:30, Jason has eaten breakfast and brushed his teeth. Then, Jason gets dressed. At 7:00, he packs his backpack and is ready to go. His bus does not come until 7:30. So, Jason takes the dog for a walk. He can't wait to get to school!

What time does Jason's bus come?

What time does Jason get up in the morning?

What time does Jason pack his backpack?

By what time has Jason brushed his teeth?

Lesson 4.2 Reading Paragraphs About Time

Read the story and the questions. Write the answers.

 Fay's class is going on a field trip. The bus leaves at 9:00 in the morning. They will get to the zoo at 9:30. The class will see the tigers and lions first. At 12:30 in the afternoon, the class will eat lunch. Then, they will watch the dolphin show. Fay's class will get on the bus at 3:00. Fay will see her grandma in the evening. She will tell her all about the day.

What time does the bus leave for the zoo? _____

During which time of day will
the class watch the dolphin show? _____

What time will the class get to the zoo? _____

During which time of day will Fay
tell her grandma about the trip? _____

What time will Fay and her class eat lunch? _____

What time will the class leave the zoo? _____

During which time of day will
the class see the lions and tigers? _____

Lesson 4.2 Reading Paragraphs About Time

Read the story and the questions. Write the answers.

Sarah and Dad are working at the park. They get to the park at 10:00. In the morning, Sarah picks up trash and Dad paints picnic tables. At 11:30, they eat lunch. In the afternoon, Sarah plants flowers and Dad builds a wheelchair ramp. At 3:00, they finish their jobs. Sarah and Dad have had a busy day.

What time do Sarah and Dad get to the park?

_____

During which time of day does Sarah plant flowers?

_____

During which time of day does Dad paint?

_____

What time do Sarah and Dad finish working?

_____

What time do Sarah and Dad eat lunch? _____

Check What You Learned

Reading About Time

Read the story and the questions. Show the answers on the clocks.

Lynn is invited to a pool party. She will go to the party at 11:00. At noon, they will have pizza. At 2:00, Lynn and her friends will swim in the pool. Lynn will go home at 4:30.

What time will Lynn go to the pool party?

What time will Lynn go home?

Read the story and the questions. Write the answers.

Kate and Chad go to the fair in the morning. They see the horse show at 10:00. Then, they pet the goats. At 12:30, they eat lunch. They play games and go on rides in the afternoon.

What time do Kate and Chad eat lunch? _____

During which time of day do they play games?

_____

Check What You Know

Writing About Time

Write a sentence to go with the picture. Tell the time of day.

| **morning** | **afternoon** | **evening** | **night** |

_____

_____

Write a sentence to go with the picture. Tell the time shown.

_____

_____

Make a schedule for Tom. Show the time he will do each thing.

| Wash dog |  |
| Feed fish  |  |

Lesson 5.1 Writing Sentences About Time of Day

What do you do in the morning? Write a sentence.

_____

_____

What do you do in the afternoon? Write a sentence.

_____

_____

What do you do in the evening? Write a sentence.

_____

_____

Draw a picture of your favorite time of day. Write the time of day.

Lesson 5.1 Writing Sentences About Time of Day

Write sentences to go with the pictures. Tell the time of day.

morning	afternoon	evening	night

_____

_____

_____

_____

_____

_____

_____

_____

_____

Lesson 5.2 Writing Sentences About Time

What time do you get up for school? Write a sentence. Tell the time.

_____

_____

What time do you eat lunch? Write a sentence. Tell the time.

_____

_____

What time do you go to bed? Write a sentence. Tell the time.

_____

_____

Draw a picture of your favorite thing to do during the day. Write the time you do it.

Lesson 5.2 Writing Sentences About Time

Write sentences to go with the pictures. Tell the time shown.

_____

_____

_____

_____

_____

_____

Lesson 5.2 Writing Sentences About Time

Write sentences to go with the pictures. Tell the time shown.

_____

_____

_____

_____

_____

_____

Lesson 5.3 Making a Time Schedule: Sunday

Look at Mike's schedule. Write the times he will do these things.

Mike's Schedule for Sunday	
Wake up	:
Eat breakfast	:
Go for a bike ride	:
Eat a snack	:
Play the drums	:
Go swimming	:

Lesson 5.3 Making a Time Schedule: Monday

Look at Trisha's schedule. Draw the times she will do these things.

Trisha's Schedule for Monday	
Wake up	(clock)
Go to the fair	(clock)
Fly a kite	(clock)
Read a book	(clock)
Play the piano	(clock)
Look at the moon	(clock)

Lesson 5.3 Making a Time Schedule: Tuesday

Look at Mom's schedule. Show the times she will do these things.

Mom's Schedule for Tuesday	
Drink coffee	
Brush teeth	
Go to work	
Eat lunch	
Drive home	
Walk dog	

Lesson 5.3 Making a Time Schedule: Wednesday

Look at Dad's schedule. Write the times he will do these things.

Dad's Schedule for Wednesday	
Eat breakfast	_____ o'clock
Read the newspaper	_____ thirty
Go on a bike ride	_____ o'clock
Go to work	_____ thirty
Make dinner	_____ o'clock
Play baseball	_____ thirty

Lesson 5.3 Making a Time Schedule: Thursday

Look at this family's schedule. Write the times they will do these things.

Our Family's Schedule for Thursday	
Eat breakfast	_____ :30
Go to the pet store	_____ :00
Go on a hike	_____ :00
Play with the dog	_____ :00
Eat dinner	_____ :30
Brush teeth	_____ :30

Lesson 5.3 Making a Time Schedule: Friday

Look at this schedule. Write a time to do each thing.

My Schedule for Friday	
Get up	_____
Eat breakfast	_____
Go to school	_____
Play games	_____
Do homework	_____
Brush teeth	_____

Lesson 5.3 Making a Time Schedule: Saturday

Make a schedule for Saturday. Draw pictures of things you will do.
Write a time to do each thing.

My Schedule for Saturday	
	_____
	_____
	_____
	_____
	_____
	_____

Check What You Learned

Writing About Time

Write a sentence to go with the picture.
Tell the time of day.

morning	afternoon	evening	night

_____

_____

Write a sentence to go with the
picture. Tell the time shown.

_____

_____

_____

Make a schedule for Beth. Show the time she will do each thing.

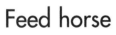 Paint	
 Feed horse	

Final Test Chapters 1–5

Look at the calendar. Write the missing days of the week. Answer the questions.

AUGUST

Sunday			Wednesday	Thursday		Saturday
				1	2	3
4	5	6	7	8	9	10
11	12	13	14	15	16	17
18	19	20	21	22	23	24
25	26	27	28	29	30	31

1. On what day of the week is August 14?

   _____

2. On what date will the family go to a baseball game?

   _____

3. On what day of the week is there a birthday party?

   _____

Final Test Chapters 1–5

Circle the events that often happen in the morning.

Alarm clocks ring.   Adults make breakfast.

Stores close for the day.   Children wake up.

Circle the events that often happen in the evening.

Everyone sleeps.   Children do homework.

The sun goes down.   Families eat breakfast.

Circle the time that best completes each sentence.

Chandra had piano lessons at _____ in the afternoon.

four o'clock   seven o'clock   eleven o'clock

The stars were shining brightly outside Benji's window.
It was _____ at night.

five thirty   six thirty   nine thirty

Mr. Maki has dance lessons at _____ in the evening.

twelve o'clock   two thirty   seven o'clock

Final Test Chapters 1–5

Circle the time for each clock.

ten o'clock   eleven o'clock

two o'clock   twelve o'clock

one o'clock   four o'clock

twelve o'clock   six o'clock

Read the clocks. Write the times in two ways.

_____ o'clock

_____:00

_____ o'clock

_____:00

_____ o'clock

_____:00

_____ o'clock

_____:00

Final Test Chapters 1–5

Circle the time for each clock.

three thirty   four thirty

one thirty   ten thirty

one thirty   twelve thirty

two thirty   three thirty

Read the clocks. Write the times in two ways.

_____ thirty

_____:30

two _____

2:_____

_____ thirty

_____:30

eleven _____

11:_____

Final Test Chapters 1–5

Read the story and the questions. Circle the answers.

Tomorrow is the Fourth of July! Sunny and Cho will go to the parade in the morning. The parade begins at 10:00. Sunny will wave at the clowns. Cho will catch candy. They will hear the bands play. In the afternoon, they will swim at the lake. They will have dinner at 5:30. In the evening, they will go for a boat ride. Then, at 9:00, the fireworks will go off. It sounds like a fun day for Sunny and Cho.

What time does the parade begin?	5:30	9:00	10:00
During which time of day will Sunny and Cho swim?	morning	afternoon	evening
What time is dinner?	5:30	10:00	9:00
During which time of day will Sunny and Cho take a boat ride?	afternoon	evening	morning

Draw hands on the clock to show what time the fireworks begin.

Final Test Chapters 1–5

Write sentences to go with the pictures. Tell the time shown.

_____   _____

_____   _____

_____   _____

_____   _____

Make a schedule for Felipe. Show the time he will do each thing.

Go sledding		
Play the drum		

Scoring Record for Posttests, Mid-Test, and Final Test

Chapter Posttest	Your Score	Performance			
		Excellent	Very Good	Fair	Needs Improvement
1	___ of 9	9	8	6–7	5 or fewer
2	___ of 10	10	9	7–8	6 or fewer
3	___ of 18	18	16–17	12–15	11 or fewer
4	___ of 4	4	4	3	2 or fewer
5	___ of 4	4	4	3	2 or fewer
Mid-Test	___ of 18	18	16–17	12–15	11 or fewer
Final Test	___ of 44	44	40–43	31–39	30 or fewer

Record your test score in the Your Score column. See where your score falls in the Performance columns. If your score is fair or needs improvement, review the chapter material again.

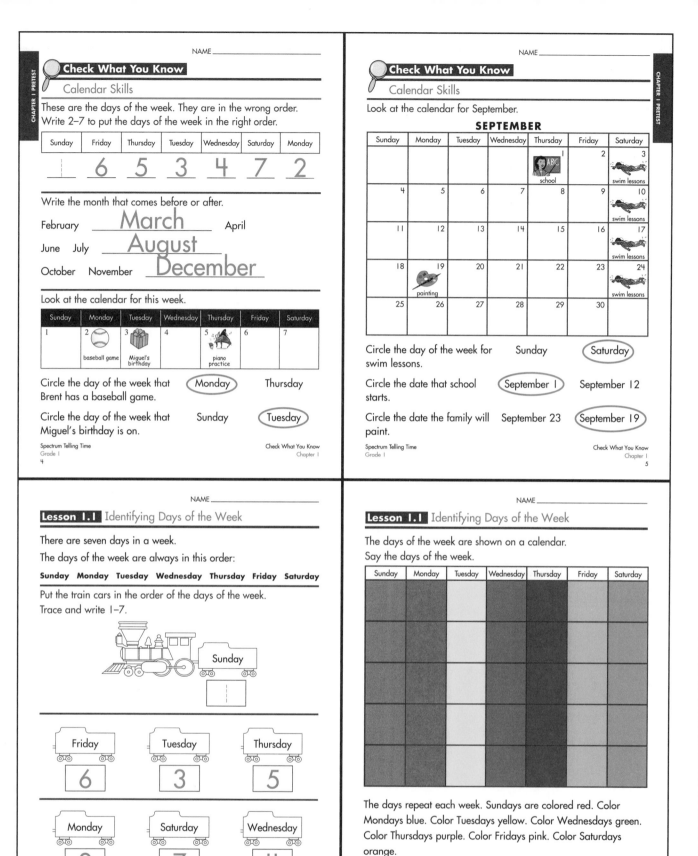

Lesson 1.2 Identifying Months of the Year

There are 12 months in the year.

The months of the year are always in this order:

January	February	March
April	May	June
July	August	September
October	November	December

Put the months in the correct order. Trace and write 1–12.

1 January	6 June	11 November
3 March	4 April	2 February
5 May	8 August	7 July
12 December	10 October	9 September

Chapter 1, Lesson 2
Calendar Skills

Lesson 1.2 Identifying Months of the Year

Say the months of the year:

January February March April May June
July August September October November December

Write the month that comes before or after.

September October November

May **June** July

February March **April**

August September **October**

July **August** September

May June July

Chapter 1, Lesson 2
Calendar Skills
9

Lesson 1.3 Reading a Calendar

Look at Sam's calendar. Tell what is happening this week.

Sunday	Monday	Tuesday	Wednesday	Thursday	Friday	Saturday
1 library	2 softball practice	3 Miguel's birthday	4	5	6 doctor appointment	7

On what day does Sam play softball?

Monday

On what day does Sam celebrate his friend's birthday?

Tuesday

On what day does Sam go to the library?

Sunday

On what day does Sam play the piano?

Thursday

On what day does Sam go to the doctor?

Friday

On what days does Sam have nothing to do?

Wednesday and **Saturday**

Chapter 1, Lesson 3
Calendar Skills

Lesson 1.3 Reading a Calendar

Look at Bella's calendars. Tell what is happening each month.

APRIL

Sunday	Monday	Tuesday	Wednesday	Thursday	Friday	Saturday
1	2	3	4	5	6	7
8	9	10	11	12	13	14
15	16	17	18	19	20	21
22 29	23 30	24	25	22	27	28

JULY

Sunday	Monday	Tuesday	Wednesday	Thursday	Friday	Saturday
1	2	3	4	5	6	7
8	9	10	11	12	13	14
15	16	17	18	19	20	21
22 29	23 30	24 31	25	22	27	28

SEPTEMBER

Sunday	Monday	Tuesday	Wednesday	Thursday	Friday	Saturday
1	2	3	4	5	6	7
8	9	10	11	12	13	14
15	16	17	18	19	20	21
22 29	23 30	24	25	22	27	28

In what month does Bella celebrate her birthday?

April

In what month does Bella start school?

September

In what month does Bella go to the beach?

July

Chapter 1, Lesson 3
Calendar Skills
11

Spectrum Telling Time

Grade 1

Answer Key

Lesson 1.3 Reading a Calendar

Mom plans family activities for July. Answer the questions.

JULY

Sunday	Monday	Tuesday	Wednesday	Thursday	Friday	Saturday
				1	2	3 camp
4	5	6	7 game night	8	9	10
11	12 zoo	13	14 game night	15	16	17
18	19	20	21 game night	22 karate	23	24
25	26	27	28 game night	29	30	31

When is game night? Friday (Wednesday)

When is karate? Tuesday (Thursday)

When is camping? July 13 (July 3)

When is the trip to the zoo? (July 12) July 20

Spectrum Telling Time
Grade 1
12

Chapter 1, Lesson 3
Calendar Skills

Lesson 1.4 Using a Calendar

Josie has swimming lessons on Monday. She has singing lessons on Friday. Help Josie plan the rest of her week by following the directions below.

Sunday	Monday	Tuesday	Wednesday	Thursday	Friday	Saturday
	swim lessons				singing lessons	

Josie wants to play kickball with her friends.

On the calendar, draw a ball on the day Josie will play kickball.

Write the day Josie will play kickball. _____

Josie wants to practice her dance moves with Dan.

On the calendar, write the word **dance** on the day Josie will practice dancing.

Write the day Josie will practice dancing. _____

Josie wants to write a story.

On the calendar, draw a pencil on the day Josie will write a story.

Write the day Josie will write a story. _____

Answers will vary but should include correct images and words on the calendar and days of the week that correlate to the calendar.

Spectrum Telling Time
Grade 1

Chapter 1, Lesson 4
Calendar Skills
13

💡 Check What You Learned

Calendar Skills

Write the missing days of the week.

<u>Sunday</u>, Monday, <u>Tuesday</u>, <u>Wednesday</u>, <u>Thursday</u>, Friday, <u>Saturday</u>

Write the month that comes before or after.

<u>October</u> November December

January February <u>March</u>

Look at Tom's calendar.

FEBRUARY

Sunday	Monday	Tuesday	Wednesday	Thursday	Friday	Saturday
1	2	3	4	5	6	7
8	9	10	11	12	13	14
15	16	17	18	19	20	21
22	23	24	25	22	27	28

When will Tom leave on a trip?

(Saturday) Sunday

When will Tom go to a party?

February 9 (February 19)

Spectrum Telling Time
Grade 1
14

Check What You Learned
Chapter 1

🔍 Check What You Know

Time of Day

Label each event with the time of day it is most likely to happen. Use **M** for morning, **A** for afternoon, **E** for evening, and **N** for night.

N Everyone sleeps.

M Families eat breakfast.

N Stars come out in the sky.

M School buses take children to school.

E The sun goes down.

A Children come home from school.

Circle the time that best completes each sentence.

I had a doctor's appointment at _____ in the morning. The sun was just rising. one o'clock (ten o'clock)

The first graders ate lunch at _____ in the afternoon. (twelve thirty) five o'clock

The play started at _____ in the evening. two thirty (seven thirty)

Clara went to bed at _____ at night. five o'clock (nine o'clock)

Spectrum Telling Time
Grade 1

Check What You Know
Chapter 2
15

Lesson 2.1 Understanding Time of Day: Morning

Morning is the beginning of the day.

The sun comes up in the morning.

People wake up in the morning.

Circle the events that often happen in the morning.

Children come home from school.   (Alarm clocks ring.)

Everyone gets ready for bed.   (Families eat breakfast.)

(School buses take children to school.)   (Adults leave for work.)

Draw a picture of something you do in the morning.

Drawings will vary.

Lesson 2.2 Understanding Time of Day: Afternoon

Afternoon is the part of the day between morning and when the sun sets.

The sun is still in the sky in the afternoon.

People eat lunch in the afternoon.

Circle the events that often happen in the afternoon.

(Students go out for recess.)   (Children come home from school.)

People wake up.   (Teachers teach lessons.)

(Children have play dates.)   Adults leave for work.

Draw a picture of something you do in the afternoon.

Drawings will vary.

Lesson 2.3 Understanding Time of Day: Evening

Evening is near the end of the day.

The sun goes down in the evening.

Families often spend time indoors in the evening.

Circle the events that often happen in the evening.

(People eat dinner.)   People eat breakfast.

(Families play board games.)   (Children do homework.)

Children play tag.   Alarm clocks ring.

Draw a picture of something you do in the evening.

Drawings will vary.

Lesson 2.4 Understanding Time of Day: Night

Night is at the very end of the day.

The sky is dark at night.

People sleep at night.

Circle the events that often happen at night.

(Parents read to children.)   Adults make breakfast.

(Stores close for the day.)   (Stars come out in the sky.)

Children play sports.   Teachers teach lessons.

Draw a picture of something you do in the evening.

Drawings will vary.

Spectrum Telling Time
Grade 1

Answer Key

Lesson 2.5 Understanding Clock Time With Time of Day

When telling time, it is important to know what part of the day it is, too. That's because we use each time twice a day. For example, we have 4:00 in the morning and 4:00 in the afternoon. Very different things are likely to happen at those two times of day.

four o'clock in the morning   four o'clock in the afternoon

What do you do at each time? Write your answer on the line.

At twelve thirty in the afternoon, I _____.

At twelve thirty at night, I _____.

At seven o'clock in the morning, I _____.

At seven o'clock in the evening, I _____.

Answers will vary.

Lesson 2.6 Combining Clock Time With Time of Day

Circle the time of day that fits best with the event described.

Breakfast is served at six thirty _____.
(in the morning)   in the evening

The sun goes down at five thirty _____.
in the morning   (in the evening)

My family goes to the beach at two o'clock _____.
(in the afternoon)   at night

Eli gets ready for bed at eight o'clock _____.
in the morning   (at night)

Our class has spelling lessons at one thirty _____.
(in the afternoon)   at night

Lesson 2.6 Combining Clock Time With Time of Day

Finish each sentence. Then, draw a picture of something you do at that time.

At _seven o'clock_ in the morning, I _____.

At _____ in the afternoon, I _____.

Answers and drawings will vary.

At _____ in the evening, I _____.

At _____ at night, I _____.

Check What You Learned

Time of Day

Label each event with the time of day it is most likely to happen. Use **M** for morning, **A** for afternoon, **E** for evening, and **N** for night.

E Families eat dinner.   M Alarm clocks ring.
N The moon shines brightly.   A Students eat lunch.
M Adults leave for work.   A Children come home from school.

Circle the time that best completes each sentence.

Grandma got up at _____ in the morning. The sun was just rising.
(six thirty)   nine thirty   twelve thirty

Jerome had soccer practice at _____ in the afternoon.
(three o'clock)   six o'clock   eleven o'clock

Uncle Peter played tennis until _____ in the evening.
three thirty   (seven thirty)   ten thirty

Sasha woke up in the middle of the night. It was _____.
six o'clock   eight o'clock   (twelve o'clock)

CHAPTER 2 POSTTEST

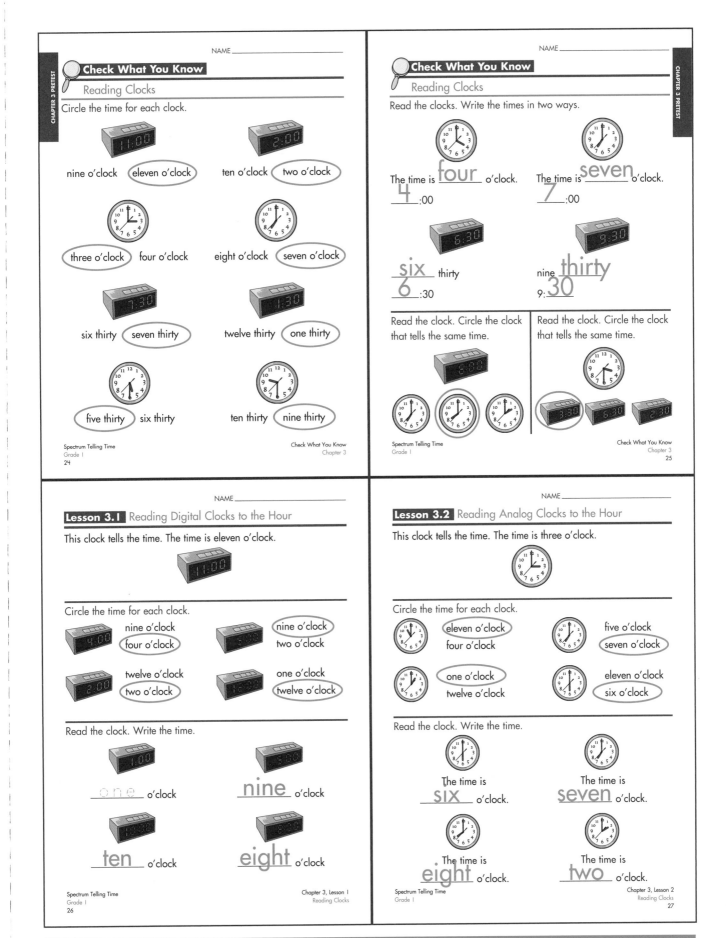

NAME _____

Check What You Know

Reading Clocks

Circle the time for each clock.

nine o'clock (eleven o'clock)

ten o'clock (two o'clock)

(three o'clock) four o'clock

eight o'clock (seven o'clock)

six thirty (seven thirty)

twelve thirty (one thirty)

(five thirty) six thirty

ten thirty (nine thirty)

Spectrum Telling Time
Grade 1
24

Check What You Know
Chapter 3

NAME _____

Check What You Know

Reading Clocks

Read the clocks. Write the times in two ways.

The time is _four_ o'clock.
_4_:00

The time is _seven_ o'clock.
_7_:00

six thirty
_6_:30

nine _thirty_
9:_30_

Read the clock. Circle the clock that tells the same time.

Read the clock. Circle the clock that tells the same time.
(3:30)

Spectrum Telling Time
Grade 1
25

Check What You Know
Chapter 3

NAME _____

Lesson 3.1 Reading Digital Clocks to the Hour

This clock tells the time. The time is eleven o'clock.

Circle the time for each clock.

nine o'clock
(four o'clock)

(nine o'clock)
two o'clock

twelve o'clock
(two o'clock)

one o'clock
(twelve o'clock)

Read the clock. Write the time.

one o'clock

nine o'clock

ten o'clock

eight o'clock

Spectrum Telling Time
Grade 1
26

Chapter 3, Lesson 1
Reading Clocks

NAME _____

Lesson 3.2 Reading Analog Clocks to the Hour

This clock tells the time. The time is three o'clock.

Circle the time for each clock.

(eleven o'clock)
four o'clock

five o'clock
(seven o'clock)

(one o'clock)
twelve o'clock

eleven o'clock
(six o'clock)

Read the clock. Write the time.

The time is _six_ o'clock.

The time is _seven_ o'clock.

The time is _eight_ o'clock.

The time is _two_ o'clock.

Spectrum Telling Time
Grade 1
27

Chapter 3, Lesson 2
Reading Clocks

Spectrum Telling Time

Grade 1

Answer Key

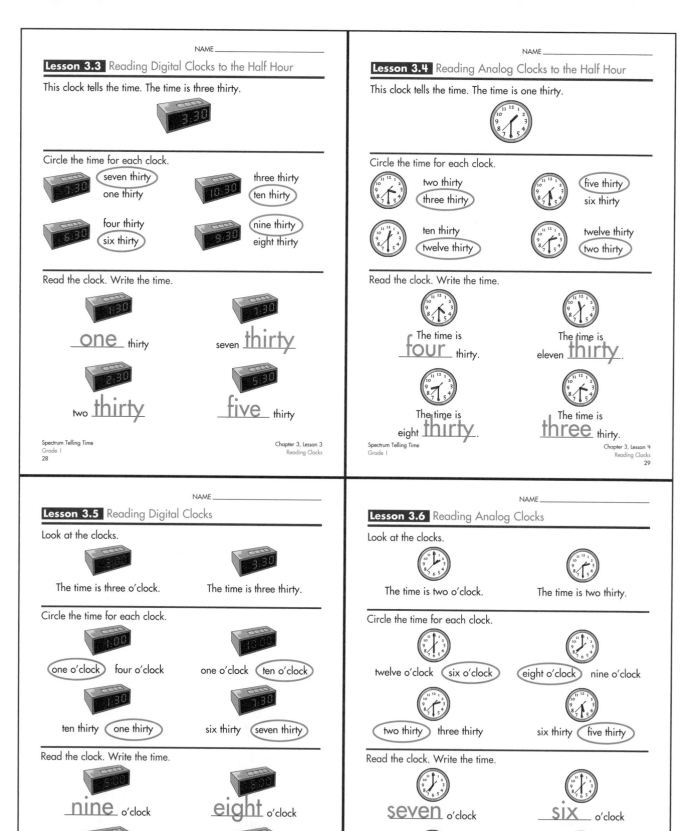

Lesson 3.3 Reading Digital Clocks to the Half Hour

This clock tells the time. The time is three thirty.

Circle the time for each clock.

seven thirty
(one thirty)

(three thirty)
ten thirty

four thirty
(six thirty)

(nine thirty)
eight thirty

Read the clock. Write the time.

___one___ thirty

seven __thirty__

two __thirty__

__five__ thirty

Lesson 3.4 Reading Analog Clocks to the Half Hour

This clock tells the time. The time is one thirty.

Circle the time for each clock.

two thirty
(three thirty)

(five thirty)
six thirty

ten thirty
(twelve thirty)

twelve thirty
(two thirty)

Read the clock. Write the time.

The time is
__four__ thirty.

The time is
eleven __thirty__.

The time is
eight __thirty__

The time is
__three__ thirty.

Lesson 3.5 Reading Digital Clocks

Look at the clocks.

The time is three o'clock.

The time is three thirty.

Circle the time for each clock.

(one o'clock)   four o'clock

one o'clock   (ten o'clock)

ten thirty   (one thirty)

six thirty   (seven thirty)

Read the clock. Write the time.

__nine__ o'clock

__eight__ o'clock

__two__ thirty

five __thirty__

Lesson 3.6 Reading Analog Clocks

Look at the clocks.

The time is two o'clock.

The time is two thirty.

Circle the time for each clock.

twelve o'clock   (six o'clock)

(eight o'clock)   nine o'clock

(two thirty)   three thirty

six thirty   (five thirty)

Read the clock. Write the time.

__seven__ o'clock

__six__ o'clock

twelve __thirty__

__three__ thirty

Lesson 3.7 Reading Digital and Analog Clocks to the Hour

Read the clock. Circle the clock that tells the same time.

Read the clock. Circle the clock that tells the same time.

Read the clock. Circle the clock that tells the same time.

Lesson 3.7 Reading Digital and Analog Clocks to the Hour

Read the clock. Circle the clock that tells the same time.

Read the clock. Circle the clock that tells the same time.

Read the clock. Circle the clock that tells the same time.

Lesson 3.7 Reading Digital and Analog Clocks to the Hour

Read the time on the first clock. Draw the hands to show this time on the second clock.

Lesson 3.7 Reading Digital and Analog Clocks to the Hour

Read the time on the first clock. Write this time on the second clock.

6:00   7:00

8:00   2:00

3:00   11:00

1:00   4:00

Spectrum Telling Time

Answer Key

Grade 1

Lesson 3.7 Reading Digital and Analog Clocks to the Hour

Read the time on the first clock. Draw the hands to show this time on the second clock.

Read the time on the first clock. Write this time on the second clock.

Lesson 3.7 Reading Digital and Analog Clocks to the Hour

Read the time on the first clock. Draw the hands to show this time on the second clock. Then, write the time in two ways.

It is **four** o'clock.
4 :00

It is **nine** o'clock.
9 :00

Read the time on the first clock. Write this time on the second clock. Then, write the time in two ways.

It is **one** o'clock.
1 :00

It is **four** o'clock.
4 :00

Lesson 3.8 Reading Digital and Analog Clocks to the Half Hour

Read the clock. Circle the clock that tells the same time.

Read the clock. Circle the clock that tells the same time.

Read the clock. Circle the clock that tells the same time.

Lesson 3.8 Reading Digital and Analog Clocks to the Half Hour

Read the clock. Circle the clock that tells the same time.

Read the clock. Circle the clock that tells the same time.

Read the clock. Circle the clock that tells the same time.

Lesson 3.8 Reading Digital and Analog Clocks
to the Half Hour

Read the time on the first clock. Draw the hands to show this time on the second clock.

Spectrum Telling Time
Grade 1
40

Chapter 3, Lesson 8
Reading Clocks

Lesson 3.8 Reading Digital and Analog Clocks
to the Half Hour

Read the time on the first clock. Write this time on the second clock.

Spectrum Telling Time
Grade 1

Chapter 3, Lesson 8
Reading Clocks
41

Lesson 3.8 Reading Digital and Analog Clocks
to the Half Hour

Read the time on the first clock. Draw the hands to show this time on the second clock.

Read the time on the first clock. Write this time on the second clock.

Spectrum Telling Time
Grade 1
42

Chapter 3, Lesson 8
Reading Clocks

Lesson 3.8 Reading Digital and Analog Clocks
to the Half Hour

Read the time on the first clock. Draw the hands to show this time on the second clock. Then, write the time in two ways.

It is ___nine___ thirty.
___9___:30

It is six ___thirty___.
6:___30___

Read the time on the first clock. Write this time on the second clock. Then, write the time in two ways.

It is eleven ___thirty___.
11:___30___

It is ___eight___ thirty.
___8___:30

Spectrum Telling Time
Grade 1

Chapter 3, Lesson 8
Reading Clocks
43

Spectrum Telling Time
Grade 1

Answer Key

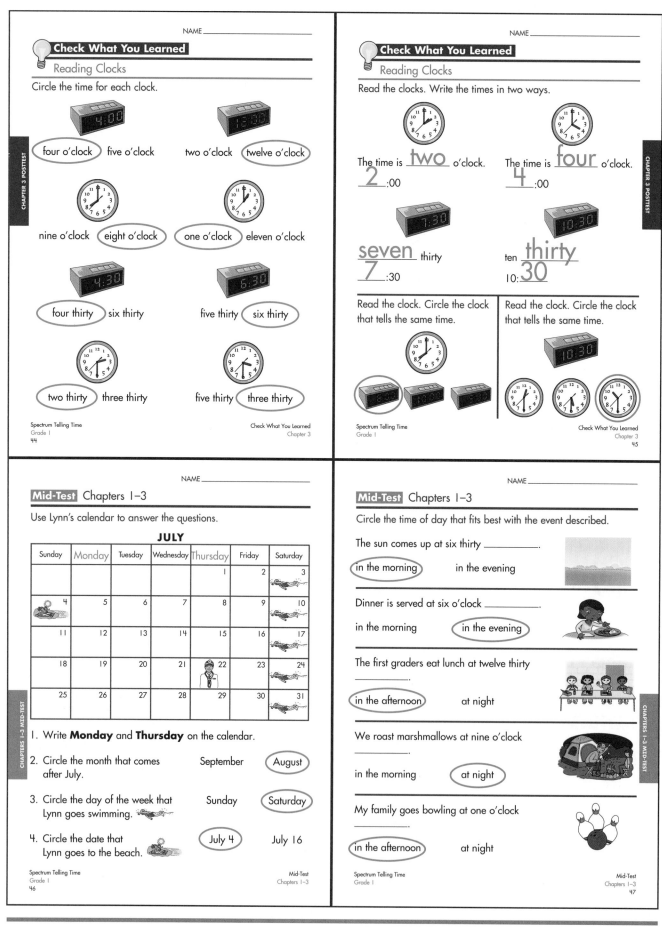

Mid-Test Chapters 1-3

Circle the time for each clock.

  two o'clock
(three o'clock)

  (ten thirty)
one thirty

  (seven o'clock)
eight o'clock

  six thirty
(five thirty)

Read the clock. Circle the clock that tells the same time.

Read the clock. Circle the clock that tells the same time.

Read the time on the first clock. Show this time on the second clock.

   6:00   3:30

Spectrum Telling Time
Grade 1
48

Mid-Test
Chapters 1-3

Check What You Know

Reading About Time

Read the sentence. Write the time.

Sam's soccer game begins at 2:30.   __two__ thirty

The school bell rings at 3:00.   three __o'clock__

Mom goes to work at 6:30.   six __thirty__

Read the sentence. Show the time on the clock.

The movie begins at 4:00.   4:00

Dad makes dinner at 5:30.

Read the story and the questions. Show the answers on the clocks.

Juan meets his friends at 1:30 at the park. They play baseball until 3:30. Then, Juan has a snack at 4:00. Dad makes dinner. The family eats at 6:30.

What time does Juan meet his friends?

What time does Juan have a snack?

 4:00

Spectrum Telling Time
Grade 1
49

Check What You Know
Chapter 4

Lesson 4.1 Reading Sentences About Time

Read the sentence. Write the time.

Jan goes to school at 8:00.   __eight__ o'clock

Dad gets home from work at 5:30.   __five__ thirty

We eat lunch at 12:00.   twelve __o'clock__

Tony has a soccer game at 9:00.   __nine__ o'clock

We eat dinner at 6:30.   six __thirty__

Mom has yoga at 10:30.   __ten__ thirty

The library closes at 8:30.   eight __thirty__

The party is at 3:00.   three __o'clock__

Spectrum Telling Time
Grade 1
50

Chapter 4, Lesson 1
Reading About Time

Lesson 4.1 Reading Sentences About Time

Read the sentence. Show the time on the clock.

Mom goes to work at 9:00.   9:00

Felix gets on the bus at 8:30.   8:30

Tina has swim lessons at 4:30.

Gym class begins at 2:00.

Ben takes the dog for a walk at 6:00.   6:00

Hannah takes a bath at 7:30.

The baseball game begins at 1:00.

The parade ends at 11:30.   11:30

Spectrum Telling Time
Grade 1
51

Chapter 4, Lesson 1
Reading About Time

Lesson 4.2 Reading Paragraphs About Time

Read the story and the questions. Circle the answers.

Mark and Mom have a busy day. They get up at 7:00 in the morning. Mom packs their lunch to eat at the beach. Mark gets his beach toys to play with in the afternoon. Mark and Mom get into the car at 10:30. Off to the beach they go! They tell Dad they will see him for dinner at 5:00 in the evening. Mark will go to bed by 8:30.

What time do Mark and Mom get up?	5:00	8:30	(7:00)
What time will Mark and Mom see Dad?	(5:00)	10:30	6:00
During which time of day will Mark play with the beach toys?	noon	(afternoon)	evening
What time do Mark and Mom leave for the beach?	6:00	8:30	(10:30)
During which time of day will the family eat dinner?	(evening)	night	afternoon
What time will Mark go to bed?	10:30	(8:30)	6:00

Lesson 4.2 Reading Paragraphs About Time

Read the story and the questions. Show the answers on the clocks.

Jason loves going to school. His alarm rings at 6:00. By 6:30, Jason has eaten breakfast and brushed his teeth. Then, Jason gets dressed. At 7:00, he packs his backpack and is ready to go. His bus does not come until 7:30. So, Jason takes the dog for a walk. He can't wait to get to school!

What time does Jason's bus come?

What time does Jason get up in the morning?

6:00

What time does Jason pack his backpack?

By what time has Jason brushed his teeth?

6:30

Lesson 4.2 Reading Paragraphs About Time

Read the story and the questions. Write the answers.

Fay's class is going on a field trip. The bus leaves at 9:00 in the morning. They will get to the zoo at 9:30. The class will see the tigers and lions first. At 12:30 in the afternoon, the class will eat lunch. Then, they will watch the dolphin show. Fay's class will get on the bus at 3:00. Fay will see her grandma in the evening. She will tell her all about the day.

What time does the bus leave for the zoo? __9:00__

During which time of day will the class watch the dolphin show? __afternoon__

What time will the class get to the zoo? __9:30__

During which time of day will Fay tell her grandma about the trip? __evening__

What time will Fay and her class eat lunch? __12:30__

What time will the class leave the zoo? __3:00__

During which time of day will the class see the lions and tigers? __morning__

Lesson 4.2 Reading Paragraphs About Time

Read the story and the questions. Write the answers.

Sarah and Dad are working at the park. They get to the park at 10:00. In the morning, Sarah picks up trash and Dad paints picnic tables. At 11:30, they eat lunch. In the afternoon, Sarah plants flowers and Dad builds a wheelchair ramp. At 3:00, they finish their jobs. Sarah and Dad have had a busy day.

What time do Sarah and Dad get to the park?
__10:00__

During which time of day does Sarah plant flowers?
__afternoon__

During which time of day does Dad paint?
__morning__

What time do Sarah and Dad finish working?
__3:00__

What time do Sarah and Dad eat lunch? __11:30__

Answer Key

Check What You Learned

Reading About Time

Read the story and the questions. Show the answers on the clocks.

Lynn is invited to a pool party. She will go to the party at 11:00. At noon, they will have pizza. At 2:00, Lynn and her friends will swim in the pool. Lynn will go home at 4:30.

What time will Lynn go to the pool party?

What time will Lynn go home?

4:30

Read the story and the questions. Write the answers.

Kate and Chad go to the fair in the morning. They see the horse show at 10:00. Then, they pet the goats. At 12:30, they eat lunch. They play games and go on rides in the afternoon.

What time do Kate and Chad eat lunch? **12:30**

During which time of day do they play games?

afternoon

Spectrum Telling Time
Grade 1
56

Check What You Learned
Chapter 4

Check What You Know

Writing About Time

Write a sentence to go with the picture. Tell the time of day.

morning	afternoon	evening	night

Answers will vary.

_____

Write a sentence to go with the picture. Tell the time shown.

Answers will vary.

_____

Make a schedule for Tom. Show the time he will do each thing.

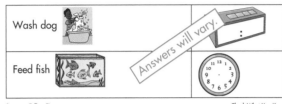

Wash dog	
Feed fish	

Answers will vary.

Spectrum Telling Time
Grade 1
57

Check What You Know
Chapter 5

Lesson 5.1 Writing Sentences About Time of Day

What do you do in the morning? Write a sentence.

Answers will vary.

_____

What do you do in the afternoon? Write a sentence.

Answers will vary.

_____

What do you do in the evening? Write a sentence.

Answers will vary.

_____

Draw a picture of your favorite time of day. Write the time of day.

Answers will vary.

Spectrum Telling Time
Grade 1
58

Chapter 5, Lesson 1
Writing About Time

Lesson 5.1 Writing Sentences About Time of Day

Write sentences to go with the pictures. Tell the time of day.

morning	afternoon	evening	night

Sentences will vary but should include one of the words from the box to express time of day.

_____

_____

Spectrum Telling Time
Grade 1
59

Chapter 5, Lesson 1
Writing About Time

Spectrum Telling Time

Grade 1

Answer Key

Lesson 5.2 Writing Sentences About Time

What time do you get up for school? Write a sentence. Tell the time.

<u>Answers will vary.</u>

_____

What time do you eat lunch? Write a sentence. Tell the time.

<u>Answers will vary.</u>

_____

What time do you go to bed? Write a sentence. Tell the time.

<u>Answers will vary.</u>

_____

Draw a picture of your favorite thing to do during the day. Write the time you do it.

Answers will vary.

Lesson 5.2 Writing Sentences About Time

Write sentences to go with the pictures. Tell the time shown.

<u>Sentences will vary but should include the time each</u>
<u>of the events took place.</u>

_____

_____

_____

Lesson 5.2 Writing Sentences About Time

Write sentences to go with the pictures. Tell the time shown.

<u>Sentences will vary but should include the time each</u>
<u>of the events took place.</u>

_____

_____

Lesson 5.3 Making a Time Schedule: Sunday

Look at Mike's schedule. Write the times he will do these things.

Mike's Schedule for Sunday

Wake up		
Eat breakfast		
Go for a bike ride		Answers will vary.
Eat a snack		
Play the drums		
Go swimming		

Lesson 5.3 Making a Time Schedule: Monday

Look at Trisha's schedule. Draw the times she will do these things.

Trisha's Schedule for Monday	
Wake up	(clock)
Go to the fair	(clock)
Fly a kite	(clock)
Read a book	(clock)
Play the piano	(clock)
Look at the moon	(clock)

Answers will vary.

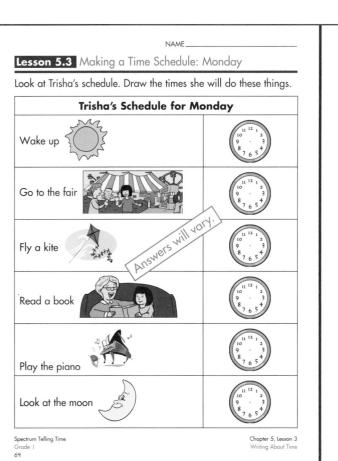

Chapter 5, Lesson 3
Writing About Time

Lesson 5.3 Making a Time Schedule: Tuesday

Look at Mom's schedule. Show the times she will do these things.

Mom's Schedule for Tuesday	
Drink coffee	(clock)
Brush teeth	(clock)
Go to work	(clock)
Eat lunch	(clock)
Drive home	(clock)
Walk dog	(clock)

Answers will vary.

Chapter 5, Lesson 3
Writing About Time
65

Lesson 5.3 Making a Time Schedule: Wednesday

Look at Dad's schedule. Write the times he will do these things.

Dad's Schedule for Wednesday	
Eat breakfast	_____ o'clock
Read the newspaper	_____ thirty
Go on a bike ride	_____ o'clock
Go to work	_____ thirty
Make dinner	_____ o'clock
Play baseball	_____ thirty

Answers will vary.

Chapter 5, Lesson 3
Writing About Time

Lesson 5.3 Making a Time Schedule: Thursday

Look at this family's schedule. Write the times they will do these things.

Our Family's Schedule for Thursday	
Eat breakfast	_____ :30
Go to the pet store	_____ :00
Go on a hike	_____ :00
Play with the dog	_____ :00
Eat dinner	_____ :30
Brush teeth	_____ :30

Answers will vary.

Chapter 5, Lesson 3
Writing About Time
67

Spectrum Telling Time
Grade 1

Answer Key

Lesson 5.3 Making a Time Schedule: Friday

Look at this schedule. Write a time to do each thing.

My Schedule for Friday	
Get up	*Answers will vary.*
Eat breakfast	
Go to school	
Play games	
Do homework	
Brush teeth	

Lesson 5.3 Making a Time Schedule: Saturday

Make a schedule for Saturday. Draw pictures of things you will do. Write a time to do each thing.

My Schedule for Saturday	
	Answers will vary.

💡 **Check What You Learned**

Writing About Time

Write a sentence to go with the picture. Tell the time of day.

morning   afternoon   evening   night

<u>Answers will vary.</u>

Write a sentence to go with the picture. Tell the time shown.

<u>Answers will vary.</u>

Make a schedule for Beth. Show the time she will do each thing.

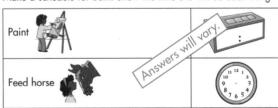

Paint	*Answers will vary.*
Feed horse	

Final Test Chapters 1–5

Look at the calendar. Write the missing days of the week. Answer the questions.

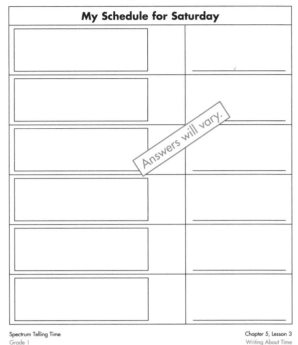

AUGUST

Sunday	Monday	Tuesday	Wednesday	Thursday	Friday	Saturday
				1	2	3
4	5	6	7	8	9	10
11	12	13	14	15	16	17
18	19	20	21	22	23	24
25	26	27	28	29	30	31

1. On what day of the week is August 14?

<u>Wednesday</u>

2. On what date will the family go to a baseball game?

<u>August 3</u>

3. On what day of the week is there a birthday party?

<u>Friday</u>

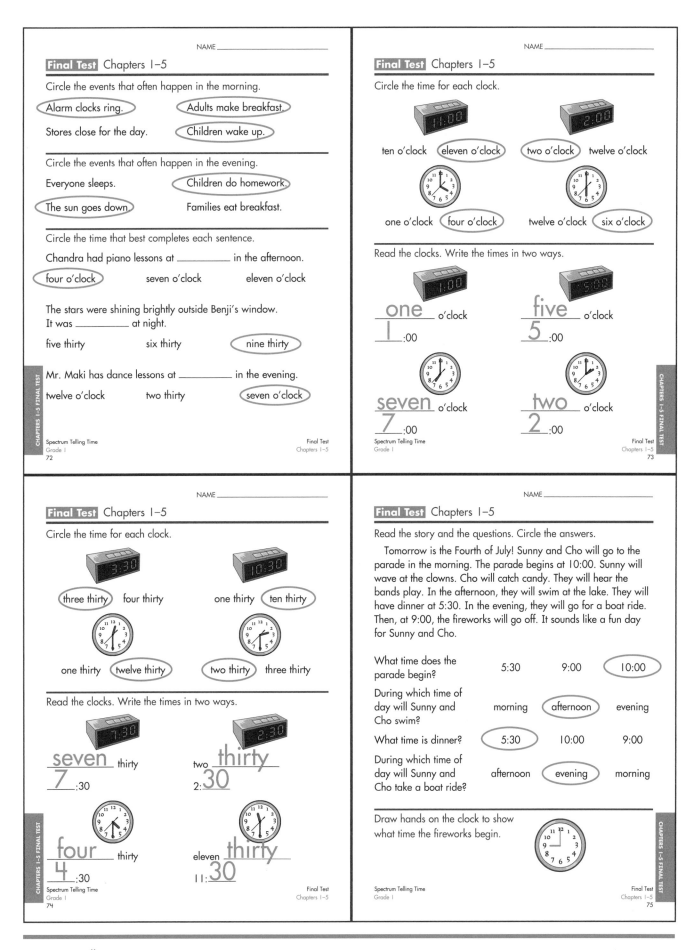

Final Test Chapters 1–5

Write sentences to go with the pictures. Tell the time shown.

_____

_____

_____

_____

_____

Answers will vary.

Make a schedule for ~~he will do~~ show the time he will do each thing.

Go sledding		
Play the drum		
